Bold Brews. Wild Hearts.

A shot of Life, Love & Everything in between

Rachael Pereira Dias

BookLeaf Publishing

India | USA | UK

Made with ❤ on the BookLeaf Publishing Platform

www.bookleafpub.in

www.bookleafpub.com

Dedication

To the ones who loved me at my best and stood by me at
my worst.
To coffee, for fueling my chaos.
To flowers, for reminding me to bloom.
And to life—messy, unpredictable, beautiful.
This one's for us.

Preface

Life brewed me strong—sometimes bitter, sometimes sweet, but always full of flavor. This book is a little bit of everything: love that lingers, losses that shape us, moments that bloom unexpectedly, and the beautiful chaos in between.

It's a collection of thoughts, stories, and reflections stirred with strength, a splash of randomness, and a whole lot of heart.

So pour yourself a cup, settle in, and let's sip through life together.

Acknowledgements

Writing this book has been a journey—one fueled by love, resilience, and, of course, countless amounts of coffee.

To my family and friends, who have cheered me on, held me up, and reminded me to keep going even when the words felt stuck—thank you. Your love is the rhythm that keeps my heart beating and my story unfolding.

To every moment of chaos, heartbreak, and joy that shaped me—thank you for giving me something to write about.

To the little things that made life brighter—sunrises, flowers, laughter, and the perfect cup of coffee—I see you. You've been my quiet companions through it all.

And finally, to you—the person holding this book. Whether you stumbled upon it or searched for it, thank you for being here. I hope these words bring you something—comfort, courage, or even just a knowing smile.

Here's to love, life, and blooming through it all.

The kind of love

You deserve to be loved like it is divine,
The kind of love that brings peace to your mind,
The kind of love that glorifies your being,
And embraces your flaws like it has never been,
The kind of love that listens to your unspoken things,
And understands your fierce soul deep within.

You deserve the kind of love,
That is unconditional and pure,
It brings you solace on your darkest night,
And dances with you when everything's alright,
A love that is gentle, a love that is kind,
A force so powerful, your heart and soul, it binds.

Hopefulness

Just like the sun that shines vibrantly after a rainy day,
I think difficult moments too can be followed with a ray
of hopefulness,
And that's beautiful.

Sunshine

I was always a big fan of sunsets,
Soft hues painting the sky,
A quiet magic that whispered—Even endings can be
beautiful.
But one day, I stood still long enough to see,
The warmth I was chasing was never out of reach.It
wasn't in the sky,
It was in me—
The sunshine was in my soul.

Therapy for my soul

Things that taste like therapy for my soul;

The aroma of freshly brewed coffee,
Mountain top views,
Cool breeze on a summer day,
Rain drops falling,
Long drives with good music,
Sunsets on quiet beaches,
Sound of waves,
Cherry Blossom trees,
You.

A midnight cry

A midnight cry,
A morning sigh,
Yet she picks herself up every time.
Like a classic masterpiece,
Her heart remains untamed,
Her mind often wanders,
In a wreck full of beauty.
Is it too much to ask for her utmost desire at this point?
Her soul longs for something boundless,
For moments that make her feel truly alive.
A midnight cry,
A morning sigh.

Human

We're only human;
We're going to rise,
We're going to fall,
We're gonna have our moments;
& We'll have it all.

We're only human;
We may have flaws,
We may falter,
We may lose confidence,
But we'll overcome it and stand tall.

We're only human;
We dream, we break,
We heal, we grow,
We carry our scars like stories untold,
Yet still, we shine, still, we glow.

We're only human!

Warmth

So I sit here,
With a hot cup of coffee,
On a winter morning.
The air is crisp, the world still quiet,
Frost lingers on the windowpane,
It's cold outside,
But warm in my heart.

Silence in sips

The world hums, a restless tide,
Honking horns, hurried footsteps,
Voices rising, crashing like waves—
Yet here I sit, untouched, unmoved.

Steam curls from my coffee cup,
A silent dance in the morning light.
The first sip—bold, unwavering,
Drowns the noise, soothes the storm.

Chaos knocks, but never enters,
Muted by this quiet rebellion.
In this stillness, I am weightless,
Whole, untangled, completely alive.

Little things

It's the little things—
The aroma of freshly ground coffee,
The mud after the first rain,
The fragrance of flowers in bloom,
And the pink sky after a stormy day.

It's the little things—
The sound of waves on a sunlit shore,
The crisp breeze that kisses your skin,
The warmth of a loved one's embrace,
And all the magic in between.

It's the little things—
That set your soul on fire.
These little things, my dear,
Are what make your heart smile.

I hope you love yourself

I hope you love yourself,
Like the flowers love the sun,
Like the stars adore the moon,
Like the waves embrace the shore—
Unquestioningly, endlessly, completely.

I hope you see yourself,
Not just in reflections, but in the way;
Laughter lingers in a room you've left,
In the warmth of the hands you've held,
And in the light you bring without even trying.

I hope you love yourself,
For the goddess that you are,
For the love you give the universe,
For the kindness your soul renders,
And for the courage your heart holds.

But most of all,
For the spirit and passion
That shine within you,
Wherever you go.

Becoming her

She's like sunshine on a cloudy day,
Like a cool breeze in the middle of May,
Like a warm hug on a winter night,
Like a ray of hope in the darkest hour.

She is light,
She is strength,
She is love, peace, and joy,
And she doesn't even know.

But watch her rise—
Soft yet unshaken,
Glowing with the fire she never saw in herself,
Blooming in the spaces she once feared.

She is light,
She is strength,
She is love, peace, and joy,
And now, she knows.

Under the Starry Sky

Under the starry night sky,
And dusky hues of blue,
With the city lights off,
And the countryside views.

Wrapped in the warmth of his love,
Stood a yearning soul,
Her heart, a quiet wildfire,
Burning bright yet beautifully whole.

The wind carried secrets untold,
Soft murmurs of dreams once lost,
But in his arms, time stood still,
And nothing felt like a cost.

In the night, her spirit sang,
A melody both tender and true,
And beneath the stars, in love's embrace,
A new story of love began anew.

She exuded magic

She exuded magic,
Just like the universe—
A quiet force, fierce and free,
Blooming even in the darkest night.

She had walked through fire,
Yet her spirit remained gold,
Not broken, but reborn,
Not lost, but endlessly whole.

She exuded magic,
Just like the universe—
Carrying light in the depths of the dark,
Holding dreams in the palms of her hands.

She was a quiet miracle,
A soft glow in the vast unknown,
Proof that even the night
Can bloom into dawn.

We belong

We belong,
Like the stars to the sky,
And the moon to the night.

We belong,
Like the sea to the shore,
And the waves to the tide.

We belong,
Like fire to the soul,
Like love that never grows old,
Like whispers of feelings, once left untold.

We belong,
Like the memories we've made—both old and new,
Each one pulling me closer,
Falling in love, again and again, with you.

Flawless

Sun-kissed skin, a story untold,
Stretch marks like rivers of courage unfold.
Wrinkles that whisper of laughter and years,
Scars that have silenced a thousand fears.

Not flaws, nor faults, nor marks of regret,
But echoes of battles we'll never forget.
Each line, each shade, each trace we bear,
A testament to the strength we wear.

So let them call them imperfections—untrue,
For every mark is a masterpiece too.
We are art, raw and rare,
Flawless in the skin we wear.

Wild & Free

And dawn paints hues so wild, so free,
Do you ever pause to wonder why
There's so much magic in the sky?

When the stars begin to softly gleam,
And the moon spills silver in a dream,
Do you ever feel the night's embrace,
As shadows dance in quiet grace?

Where whispers of enchantment call,
And love feels vast, yet light, yet small,
Do you think that's where your soul longs to be—
Lost in wonder, wild and free?

Dare to shine

17

Darling,
Let the night remind you—
Even in the deepest dark,
The stars dare to shine.

And when dawn spills its golden light,
Let it gently teach you this—
With every rising sun,
Love yourself a little more.

Whispers of ever after

When she looks back,
Her heart dances with joy,
And her eyes alight with memories—
Of a crystal-clear lake reflecting the endless blue,
Of wildflowers swaying in the wind,
Of counting stars on a cold winter night.

She remembers moonlit dances,
Soft laughter echoing in the dark,
The warmth of love wrapped around her soul,
And the magic found in the smallest moments.

Some stories fade, some moments pass,
But these—these are hers to keep,
Forever woven into the fabric of her ever-after.

Breathe, darling!

Breathe, Darling
This too shall pass.
It's just a bad phase,
Not a bad life.

The storms don't stay forever,
Nor do the restless nights.
You are stronger than this moment,
And brighter days will find you soon.

Blooming beyond the storm

She has seen the darkest nights,
Where the stars refused to shine.
She has walked through raging storms,
With trembling hands, yet a steady spine.

She knows the weight of whispered fears,
The silence heavy, the battle long.
But even in the fiercest winds,
She found her voice, she found her song.
Not every victory roars like thunder,
Some are quiet, soft, and slow—
Like the warmth of the morning sun,
Or the way wildflowers grow.

She learned to cherish stolen moments—
Laughter spilling like golden light,
The hush of waves, the scent of rain,
The magic woven in the night.

She is here, standing tall,
Not just surviving, but alive.
A story of strength, of hope, of fire—
She did not fall. **She rose.**

Embers of courage

She was not born with armor,
Nor a map to show the way.
Yet when the earth beneath her cracked,
She learned how to stay.

She has felt the weight of endings,
Stood at doors that would not budge.
She has faced the kind of silence
That only battles dare to judge.

Yet fear never broke her,
It only taught her how to stand—
Not with fury, not with rage,
But with grace at her command.

She knows courage isn't loud,
It doesn't always shout or fight.
Sometimes, it's just the choice to rise,
To breathe, to love, to hold on tight.

She is here—whole and wild,
Not because the path was kind,
But because even in the darkest hours,
She refused to leave herself behind.